D1505800

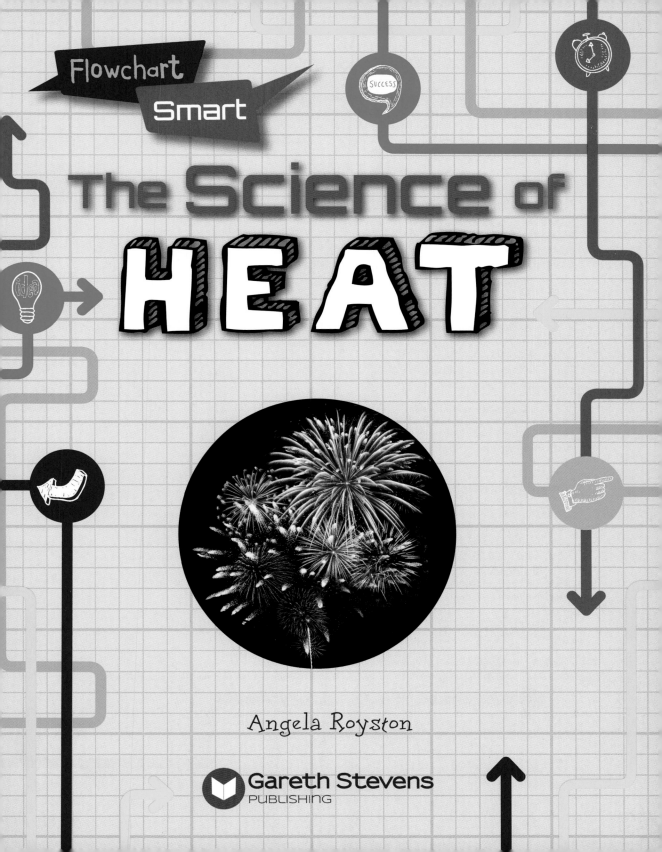

Flowchart Smart

The Science of HEAT

Angela Royston

Gareth Stevens
PUBLISHING

Please visit our website, **www.garethstevens.com**.
For a free color catalog of all our high-quality books,
call toll free 1-800-542-2595 or fax 1-877-542-2596.

Cataloging-in-Publication Data

Royston, Angela.
The science of heat / by Angela Royston.
p. cm. — (Flowchart smart)
Includes index.
ISBN 978-1-4824-4139-0 (pbk.)
ISBN 978-1-4824-4140-6 (6-pack)
ISBN 978-1-4824-4141-3 (library binding)
1. Heat — Juvenile literature. I. Royston, Angela, 1945-. II. Title.
QC256.R69 2016
536—d23

First Edition

Published in 2016 by
Gareth Stevens Publishing
111 East 14th Street, Suite 349
New York, NY 10003

Produced for Gareth Stevens by Calcium
Editors: Sarah Eason and Harriet McGregor
Designers: Paul Myerscough and Emma DeBanks

Cover art: Shutterstock: Denkcreative, Lineartestpilot.

Picture credits: Dreamstime: Hasan Can Balcioglu 14–15, Claudio Baldini 15t, Christinlola
12–13, Deymos 12b, Janaka Dharmasena 5t, Razvan Ionut Dragomirescu 18–19, Dvmsimages
26bl, Svetlana Foote 20–21, Herman118 38–39, Jatuporn79 10–11, Timothy Large 24–25,
Lucidwaters 4–5, Marazem 6–7, Heather Nicaise 27br, Piotr Skubisz 6, Hannu Viitanen 11t,
Viktorfischer 32–33; Shutterstock: 3dmotus 21b, Bloomua 45br, Djedzura 31br, Dragon
Images 33br, Fotokostic 30–31, Ioana.S 1, 26–27, Latino 36bl, Lculig 40–41, LianeM 40bl,
Mihai Maxim 44–45, Smileus 44–45t, Tutti Frutti 36–37.

Printed in the United States of America

CPSIA compliance information: Batch #CW16GS: For further information contact Gareth Stevens, New York, New York at 1-800-542-2595.

Contents

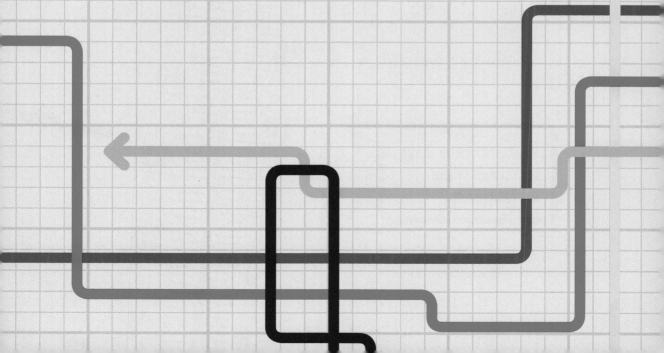

Chapter 1
Heat Causes Change

When we say that something is hot or cold, we usually mean that it is hotter or colder than our skin or our surroundings. Scientists are more precise. They use a thermometer to measure temperature using one of two scales—Fahrenheit or Celsius. The temperature tells us exactly how hot something is, but what is heat?

Heat is a form of energy and it has the ability to make something happen or change. Energy can take several forms, including light, sound, magnetism, and electricity, as well as heat. Some types of energy produce a force, which pushes or pulls an object to make it move. The energy of heat works on the smallest particles of a substance, its molecules.

This thermometer shows both scales: Celsius and Fahrenheit.

A molecule is the smallest piece of a substance that can exist and still be that substance. For example, a grain of salt is tiny, but each grain contains millions of salt molecules. A molecule of salt can be split into atoms of sodium and chlorine, but they are no longer salt!

Atoms link together to make molecules, and molecules clump together to make solids. How much space there is between the molecules determines whether a substance is solid, liquid, or gas. This is called its state of matter.

A heating coil is used in an electric oven to turn electrical energy into heat energy.

Get Smart!

Heat can change a substance completely. It can break a molecule into atoms, which combine with other molecules and atoms to produce an entirely different substance. For example, crude oil is heated and separated into different chemicals. Heat energy can change some of these chemicals into gasoline, plastic, dishwashing liquid, medicines, and many other substances.

States of Matter

Most substances can exist as a solid, liquid, or gas. Water can be solid ice, liquid water, or a gas called water vapor. The molecules are the same whatever the state of matter, but the way they behave and the spaces between the molecules are different.

In a solid, the molecules are packed close together. The molecules can vibrate, which means they move back and forth very quickly, but they cannot change position. Because the molecules are packed together, a solid keeps its shape. You must apply a force to change its shape, either by squashing, stretching, bending, or breaking it.

The molecules in a liquid have more energy than the molecules in a solid, so they vibrate more quickly and can also move around. This is why a liquid is runny and takes the shape of its container. It can be poured from one container to another, and if it is not in a container, it runs downhill or forms a pool. The surface of a liquid is always flat.

Get Smart!

Powders and granules, such as flour and salt, are solids, but they can behave like liquids. You can pour a powder from one container to another, and manufacturers use this fact to transport large quantities in tankers. To unload the powder, it is blown out of a chute.

When you pour one liquid into another, the two mix together.

The molecules in a gas have so much energy that they move very quickly and are free to move far away from one another. A gas in a container spreads out to every part of the container. In the air, the molecules move away from each other in all directions. A gas does not have a shape and it is difficult to pour, because the molecules escape into the air.

A cucumber has a tough, solid skin, which keeps the liquid juice inside from leaking out.

Get flowchart smart!

Solid, Liquid, or Gas?

Compare the way molecules in a solid, liquid, and gas behave, using a flowchart.

SUCCESS

A solid keeps its shape because *the* molecules are packed close together, with just enough room *to* vibrate.

Heat energy makes a solid's molecules vibrate more quickly and move farther apart.

In a gas, *the* molecules are free *to* move anywhere. They move into all parts of a container. Without a container they disperse *through* the air.

A liquid does not keep its shape because the molecules are farther apart and can move around more freely. The spaces between the molecules make the liquid runny.

Heat energy makes a liquid's molecules move even faster and farther apart, and the liquid becomes even hotter.

Flowchart Smart

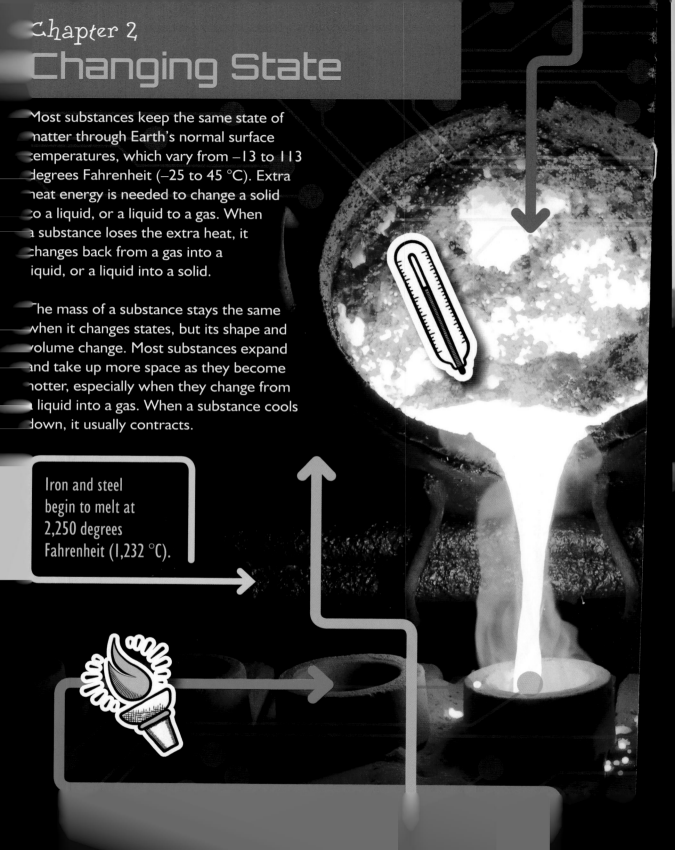

Chapter 2

Changing State

Most substances keep the same state of matter through Earth's normal surface temperatures, which vary from −13 to 113 degrees Fahrenheit (−25 to 45 °C). Extra heat energy is needed to change a solid to a liquid, or a liquid to a gas. When a substance loses the extra heat, it changes back from a gas into a liquid, or a liquid into a solid.

The mass of a substance stays the same when it changes states, but its shape and volume change. Most substances expand and take up more space as they become hotter, especially when they change from a liquid into a gas. When a substance cools down, it usually contracts.

Iron and steel begin to melt at 2,250 degrees Fahrenheit (1,232 °C).

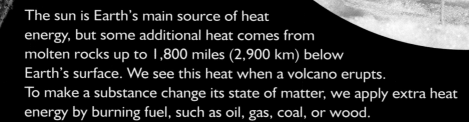

Icicles form when dripping water freezes. The icicle grows as liquid water changes to ice at the tip.

The sun is Earth's main source of heat energy, but some additional heat comes from molten rocks up to 1,800 miles (2,900 km) below Earth's surface. We see this heat when a volcano erupts. To make a substance change its state of matter, we apply extra heat energy by burning fuel, such as oil, gas, coal, or wood.

We use ice, coolers, refrigerators, and freezers to cool food and drinks to keep them fresh. To defrost food from the freezer, you simply take it out and let it warm to room temperature—about 70 degrees Fahrenheit (21 °C).

Get Smart!

Absolute zero is −459.67 degrees Fahrenheit (−273.15 °C) and is matter's lowest possible temperature. As a solid cools, its molecules vibrate less and less, until a substance at absolute zero has no heat and its molecules have no energy. They are virtually motionless. This low temperature has never been achieved, although scientists have gotten within a fraction of a degree of it. The Kelvin temperature scale uses absolute zero as its zero.

Heating Up

When enough heat energy is applied to a solid, it melts and forms a liquid. For example, chocolate melts when it is heated in a pan. As a liquid becomes warmer, it begins to evaporate and turn to gas. At a certain temperature it boils. Some solids, such as dry ice (frozen carbon dioxide), change straight into a gas from a solid. This process is called sublimation.

As a liquid warms, the molecules move more quickly. Some molecules at the surface move so fast that they escape from the liquid and float into the air. This is what happens when a puddle or a wet garment dries. The water slowly evaporates until there is none left. The hotter the liquid, the faster it evaporates. Some liquids, such as butane and gasoline, evaporate easily at room temperature. Others, such as water, take longer.

The boiling point is the temperature at which a liquid stops becoming hotter, and instead uses heat energy to change rapidly into a gas. Bubbles of gas form in a boiling liquid, rise to the surface, and escape into the air. Different substances boil at different temperatures. Metals, such as lead, iron, and copper, have very high boiling points. Lead boils at 3,180 degrees Fahrenheit (1,749 °C). Water boils at 212 degrees Fahrenheit (100 °C).

Boiling water forms bubbles of water vapor that are much hotter than the water.

Substance	State of Matter at Room Temperature	Melting Point
Olive oil	Liquid	32 degrees Fahrenheit (0 °C)
Water	Liquid	32 degrees Fahrenheit (0 °C)
Chocolate	Solid	95 degrees Fahrenheit (35 °C)
Butter	Solid	97 degrees Fahrenheit (36 °C)

Ice cream melts and becomes runny at room temperature. The outer surface warms and melts first.

Cooling Down

As a substance cools, the molecules lose energy and move closer together. A cooling gas changes into a liquid and, if it continues to cool, it may freeze to become solid. When water vapor cools it condenses to form steam, which is a mixture of water vapor and tiny water droplets.

A gas condenses when it meets something that is colder than itself. This may be a cold surface or cold air. For example, water vapor condenses on a cool bathroom mirror after a hot shower. The temperature at which a substance starts to condense is the same as its boiling point.

When hot gravy or fat cools down, it becomes thicker and forms a solid. The surface usually cools first and a skin forms. As it cools to room temperature, the whole mass may become solid. Freezing is the same process, but the word is used when a liquid cools below room temperature before it forms a solid. The freezing point is the same temperature as the melting point.

Most substances contract as they freeze, but water is different. As water freezes, it contracts as the temperature falls to 39 degrees Fahrenheit (4 °C), but then it expands as it becomes solid. This means that a lump of ice is lighter than the same volume of water, and this is why ice floats in water.

Ice contains ice crystals, which make ice less dense than liquid water.

Substance	State of Matter at Room Temperature	Freezing Point
Water	Liquid	32 degrees Fahrenheit (0 °C)
Salt water	Liquid	28 degrees Fahrenheit (–2 °C)
Mercury	Liquid	–38 degrees Fahrenheit (–39 °C)
Nitrogen	Gas	–346 degrees Fahrenheit (–210 °C)

Clouds of steam escape from a boiling kettle. Steam consists of tiny droplets of condensed water.

Get flowchart smart!

Changing Heat

Follow this flowchart to see what happens as a solid gains and loses heat energy.

A solid expands as it becomes hotter. As the molecules gain energy they vibrate faster and begin to move around, creating more space between the molecules.

As the liquid loses heat, the molecules move more slowly.

When the liquid reaches freezing point, the loss of energy speeds up the change from liquid to solid.

Flowchart Smart

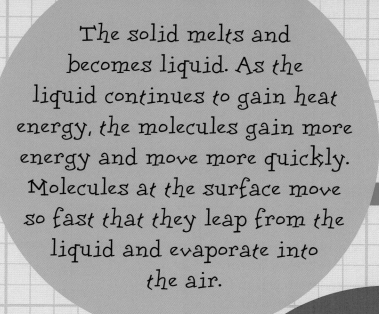

The solid melts and becomes liquid. As the liquid continues to gain heat energy, the molecules gain more energy and move more quickly. Molecules at the surface move so fast that they leap from the liquid and evaporate into the air.

Heating increases the rate of evaporation until the liquid begins to boil. Molecules near the surface evaporate. Molecules deeper in the liquid form bubbles of gas, which rise to the surface and evaporate.

As the gas loses heat energy, the molecules lose energy, move closer to one another, and form drops of condensed liquid.

SUCCESS

Chapter 3
The Water Cycle

The water cycle describes how water circulates between the land, the oceans, and the atmosphere. The water cycle is possible because water exists as a solid, liquid, and gas at Earth's regular temperatures. Around 70 percent of Earth's surface is covered with water, mostly salt water in seas and oceans, but also freshwater in rivers and lakes. Ice covers parts of the Arctic and nearly all of Antarctica, and the air close to Earth's surface contains water vapor.

The water cycle is powered by heat from the sun. The sun's heat energy warms the surface of any body of water, causing water molecules to evaporate into the air. The sun also warms the air above the water. Warm air expands and becomes less dense than the cooler air above it. The lighter, warm air rises, carrying water vapor with it. As it rises, it is replaced by denser, cooler air.

The sun warms snow in the mountains. It melts and flows in streams and rivers.

The troposphere is the lowest layer of the atmosphere, reaching around 12 miles (19 km) above sea level. As water vapor rises through the troposphere, the air becomes thinner and colder. Water vapor condenses to form clouds of tiny water droplets or ice crystals.

Water droplets move inside a cloud, collide, and form larger drops. When the drops are too heavy to float in the cloud, they fall to Earth. If the air is particularly cold, water droplets in the cloud freeze and become snowflakes. As the snowflakes fall they sometimes melt and become raindrops.

Get Smart!

Life on Earth relies on the water cycle. Rain waters the land and fills lakes and rivers. Without water, plants, including farm crops, cannot grow. People and land animals need a constant supply of drinking water.

Water on the Move

The water cycle carries water molecules from Earth's surface into the atmosphere and then returns them to the surface. On land, water drains into streams and rivers, which flow into the oceans. Molecules of water are recycled again and again. The water you drink may contain some of the same water molecules that a dinosaur drank 100 million years ago!

Water evaporates from the surface of oceans, lakes, rivers, puddles, and anywhere else that water is exposed to the sun's warmth. The warmer the air, the faster the water evaporates, which means that evaporation is fastest near the equator and slowest at the poles. In winter, the Arctic and Antarctic are so cold that there is little or no evaporation.

The water cycle redistributes water across Earth. Clouds are blown by the wind and may travel for hundreds of miles before the water they carry falls as rain or snow. Rain falls when clouds meet colder air, such as when they are pushed upward by a high mountain range. The water droplets suddenly cool and fall as rain or snow on the mountaintops.

Water that evaporates from the surface of the oceans forms clouds. Warmth and wind increase the rate of evaporation.

Get Smart!

Precipitation is water falling to Earth in any form. It includes rain, sleet, snow, and hail. It may fall as gentle rain from gray clouds or as a heavy downpour, depending on the climate. In cold winters, water falls as snow, but eventually melts. In hot places, warm oceans and hot air produce towering storm clouds. The warmer the ocean surface, the faster the water evaporates. The fast-rising air pulls in strong winds that can develop into a violent storm. As the storm strengthens and the air begins to rotate, it becomes a hurricane.

A hurricane's winds swirl violently around the central eye of the storm, in which conditions are much calmer.

Get flowchart smart!

Recycling Earth's Water

Follow the flowchart to see how the water cycle recycles Earth's water.

Heat from the sun warms the surface of the land and oceans.

→ Water molecules evaporate from Earth's surface into the air.

The sun warms the land and oceans, and the cycle starts over.

Rivers carry water back to the oceans.

SUCCESS

When warm air meets cold air, water vapor condenses and forms tiny water droplets in a cloud.

The wind blows clouds over the oceans and land. If the clouds meet a high mountain range, they are pushed upward into even colder air.

Water droplets join together to form larger water drops.

The drops fall to Earth's surface as snow, rain, or hail. Water on the land trickles into streams, lakes, and rivers.

Flowchart Smart

A substance burns when it becomes very hot and bursts into flames. Once burned, the process cannot be reversed. Burning irreversibly changes one substance into other substances, including one or more gases.

Burning is also called combustion. It occurs when a substance combines rapidly with oxygen in the air. The air is a mixture of gases and contains mostly nitrogen (about 78 percent) and oxygen (about 21 percent). Some substances combine slowly with oxygen, such as when iron rusts, but in combustion, the heat energy can make the process almost instant.

Some substances ignite and burn more easily than others. This is because their ignition temperatures are lower and they need less heat energy to burn. Firelighter cubes, paper, and kindling sticks are often used to start a fire. As they burn, they produce heat, which then lights charcoal or other fuels. These fuels burn more slowly and last longer.

To start a bonfire, kindling is lit using a match. The kindling burns and sets fire to the fuel surrounding it, such as dry wood.

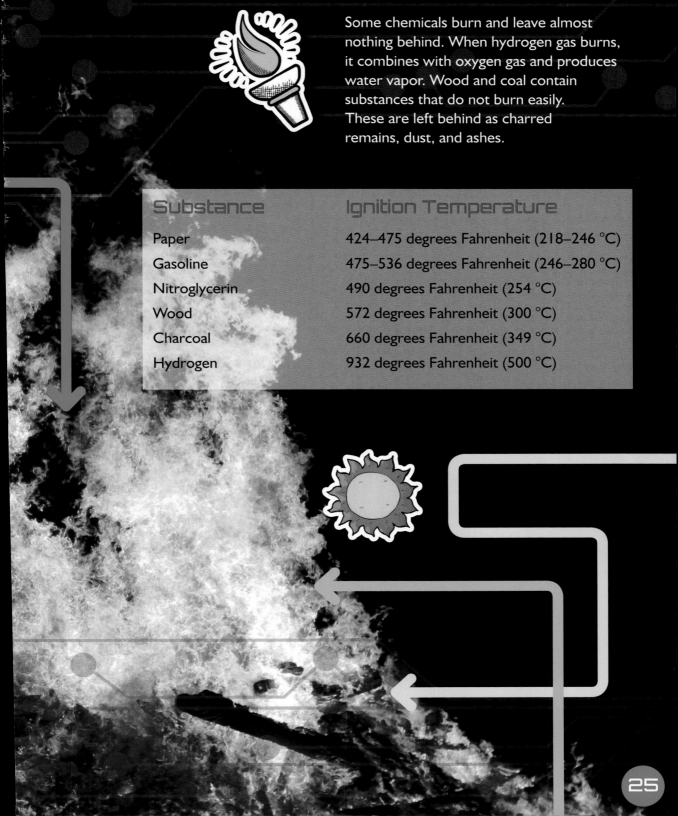

Some chemicals burn and leave almost nothing behind. When hydrogen gas burns, it combines with oxygen gas and produces water vapor. Wood and coal contain substances that do not burn easily. These are left behind as charred remains, dust, and ashes.

Substance	Ignition Temperature
Paper	424–475 degrees Fahrenheit (218–246 °C)
Gasoline	475–536 degrees Fahrenheit (246–280 °C)
Nitroglycerin	490 degrees Fahrenheit (254 °C)
Wood	572 degrees Fahrenheit (300 °C)
Charcoal	660 degrees Fahrenheit (349 °C)
Hydrogen	932 degrees Fahrenheit (500 °C)

Flames and Fuels

As a substance is heated, some of its molecules break apart and release gases. These gases can ignite and form flames. As the gases are used up, or the heat is reduced, the flames die down, although the remaining substance may burn more slowly and stay hot for some time. Substances such as stone and asbestos become very hot but they do not burn.

The more easily a material ignites, the more quickly it burns. When a firework explodes in the air, it burns briefly with a bright color. The colors in the explosion depend on the chemicals in the firework. If a firework contains copper, it burns blue. Calcium burns orange and strontium burns with a red flame.

A burning fuse ignites the gunpowder inside the firework. The gunpowder explodes and propels the firework into the air.

The gap between a candle flame and the wick is filled with vapor from the wax that has yet to ignite.

Unlike fireworks, fuels burn for a long time. Fuels include wood, dried plants, and fossil fuels, such as coal, gas, and oil. Fossil fuels are the remains of plants and creatures that lived millions of years ago. These fuels all contain carbon, which combines with oxygen to form carbon dioxide and carbon monoxide as the fuel burns.

Get Smart!

A fire needs oxygen, fuel, and heat. To put out a fire you must deprive it of one of these ingredients. Firefighters spray cold water onto a fire, which cools it and produces clouds of steam that smother the flames. Water should never be used on burning oil because it spreads the oil, and the fire. Smothering a fire deprives it of oxygen. A stove fire can be smothered using a fire blanket or a fire extinguisher. An extinguisher contains a chemical, such as potassium bicarbonate, or foam to prevent oxygen reaching the fire. Cutting down trees in the path of a forest fire deprives the fire of fuel.

A firefighting plane drops water onto a forest fire to put out the flames.

Get flowchart smart!

The Burning Process

This flowchart shows what happens as barbecue charcoal burns.

SUCCESS

Firelighter cubes or wood kindling are lit using matches or a lighter.

The burning firelighter cubes or wood pass heat energy to the charcoal.

Burned charcoal and ash remain when the fire has burned out.

As the charcoal heats up, some of its molecules break apart, producing carbon, hydrogen, and other substances.

Carbon and hydrogen molecules escape from the charcoal. They burn by combining with oxygen in the air.

Carbon dioxide and carbon monoxide gases are produced. Hydrogen combines with oxygen and releases water vapor.

After the fire has died down, the charcoal stays red-hot and can cook food.

Flowchart Smart

Chapter 5

What's Cooking?

Cooking is usually slower and more gentle than burning, but it still uses heat energy to change substances in ways that cannot be reversed. Food is cooked to make it safer and easier to eat, or to combine it with other foods to make it taste better.

Cooking changes food in different ways. A raw egg is liquid, but cooking turns the thick, clear liquid into a white solid, and thickens or solidifies the yellow-orange center. Cheese melts when it is heated. Flour expands when it is mixed with a liquid and forms a thick liquid. Vegetables, potatoes, pasta, and rice become softer when cooked.

Heat kills bacteria and other germs that can make you sick. Raw meat contains millions of bacteria, including *Salmonella* and the potentially deadly bacteria *E. coli*. To prevent food poisoning, chicken must be cooked until the internal temperature reaches at least 165 degrees Fahrenheit (74 °C). Raw eggs and unpasteurized milk can also contain bacteria and should be treated carefully.

As an egg is heated, the outer edge of the clear liquid solidifies first and turns white. Eventually, the entire egg solidifies.

Get Smart!

A microwave oven is a quick way of heating or cooking food. It emits an energy wave that is absorbed by molecules of water, fat, and sugar in the food. As these molecules become hot, they heat the rest of the food. Materials that do not contain water, such as china, glass, and plastic, remain cool, although they may absorb heat from the food.

A cell phone uses microwaves to send information over long distances. The microwaves are low intensity and only penetrate a short distance into your skin. The change in skin temperature is less than that caused by being outside on a sunny day.

Heat has transferred from the hot liquid to the bowl. Oven mitts protect the skin from damage.

Cooking Methods

There are many different ways of applying heat to food, including broiling, frying, roasting, and boiling. Cooking breaks apart the molecules in food, making them softer. This makes the food far easier to chew and digest.

Pasta, rice, and potatoes consist of long molecules of starch, called carbohydrates. Cooking and digestion break up the starch molecules into shorter molecules of sugar, which the body burns to get energy. Whole grain foods and vegetables contain fiber, which is a type of carbohydrate that the body cannot digest. Cooking vegetables softens the fiber, making it easier to chew and swallow. You need to eat plenty of fiber to keep your digestive system working properly.

Like meat, chicken, and fish, the human body is built of protein. Protein consists of long chains of amino acids. The human body's amino acids need to be constantly replaced. Cooking and digestion break down the protein chains in food into separate amino acids, which the body reassembles to make its own proteins.

Heat from a barbecue cooks the outside of the food first. Heat transfers to the inside of the food over time. If the temperature is too high, the outside can be burned and the inside still raw.

Cakes, cookies, and pastry are made by combining and cooking several different ingredients. Flour, fat, sugar, beaten eggs, and milk are mixed together to make cake batter. When eggs are beaten, the white of the egg takes in lots of air, making it light and bubbly. The cake batter is poured into a cake pan and put in a hot oven to cook. The heat melts the fat, and the ingredients blend together. As the eggs solidify, the trapped bubbles of air expand so that the whole mixture rises and forms a delicious cake!

Cupcakes are baked in an oven, but the frosting is added when the cakes are cool. The heat from a warm cake would melt the butter in the frosting.

Get flowchart smart!

What Happens When You Make a Cake?

SUCCESS

This flowchart shows how heat energy changes a list of ingredients into a cake.

Specific quantities of fat, sugar, beaten eggs, flour, and flavorings are mixed together, according to a recipe.

As the cake cools, it becomes more rigid.

The cake is cooked when the whole mixture has changed to a solid.

The cake batter is mixed thoroughly to combine the ingredients and add air. The thick liquid is poured into a cake pan.

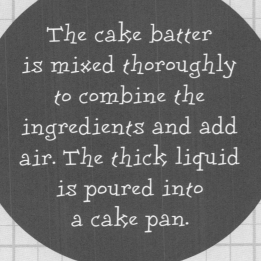

The cake pan is placed in a hot oven. Heat energy warms the cake batter.

Flour absorbs liquid and swells. Heat energy melts the fat and solidifies the particles of egg in the mixture, trapping bubbles of air.

Chapter 6

Heat Travels

Heat energy moves from hot places to cooler places. A hot object, such as a cup of coffee, cools because heat energy moves from the coffee into the cup and the air until the coffee is the same temperature as its surroundings. As a frozen object defrosts, it takes in heat energy from its surroundings until it reaches room temperature.

Heat energy travels more quickly through some materials than through others. It usually moves faster through thin objects than thick ones, but the most important factor is the material itself. Materials that transfer heat quickly are called good conductors. Materials that hold on to heat and do not transfer it easily are good insulators.

A hot drink warms you from the inside, and warm clothes keep body heat from escaping.

Metals are good conductors. Metal pans pass heat from the stove top into the food they contain, and metal heaters transfer heat to warm a room. On a hot day, metal objects may feel burning hot. This is because the heat instantly leaves the metal and enters your skin. Wooden objects are more comfortable to touch because they do not pass on heat energy as quickly.

An adobe house in New Mexico is built of traditional mud bricks to keep the rooms cool during the heat of the day.

Get Smart!

Insulation is important in both hot and cold countries. In hot countries, people want to keep the inside of their homes cool, while in cold countries they want to keep the heat inside from escaping. Traditionally, many homes in hot countries are built of baked mud, called adobe. This material is an excellent insulator. It absorbs the sun's heat during the day and releases it at night to warm the inside when the temperature drops. Wood and stone are also good insulators and are often used in cold places to keep homes warm.

Heat can travel in three different ways: conduction, convection, and radiation. Conduction takes place when heat moves directly between two materials that are touching one another. Convection occurs when a current of moving liquid or gas carries heat from one place to another. Radiation is a way that heat energy can transfer from one place to another without anything to carry it.

A metal spoon is a better conductor than a wooden one. If you put a metal spoon in a pot of cooking food, heat from the food passes directly into the scoop end of the spoon by conduction. The heat energy then passes up the spoon, until it reaches the top and burns your fingers! A wooden spoon does not transfer heat energy from the food to your fingers.

Convection moves heat in a liquid or a gas. When a liquid or gas is heated, the molecules become more active and move around more quickly. If a pot of water is heated on a stove, hot water molecules move up from the bottom toward the surface. Cooler water molecules move from the top toward the bottom where they are then heated. The water moves around in a circle called a convection current.

Radiant heat does not use molecules to transfer heat. Instead the heat travels as waves of energy. The sun's heat is radiated to Earth across 93 million miles (150 million km) of space.

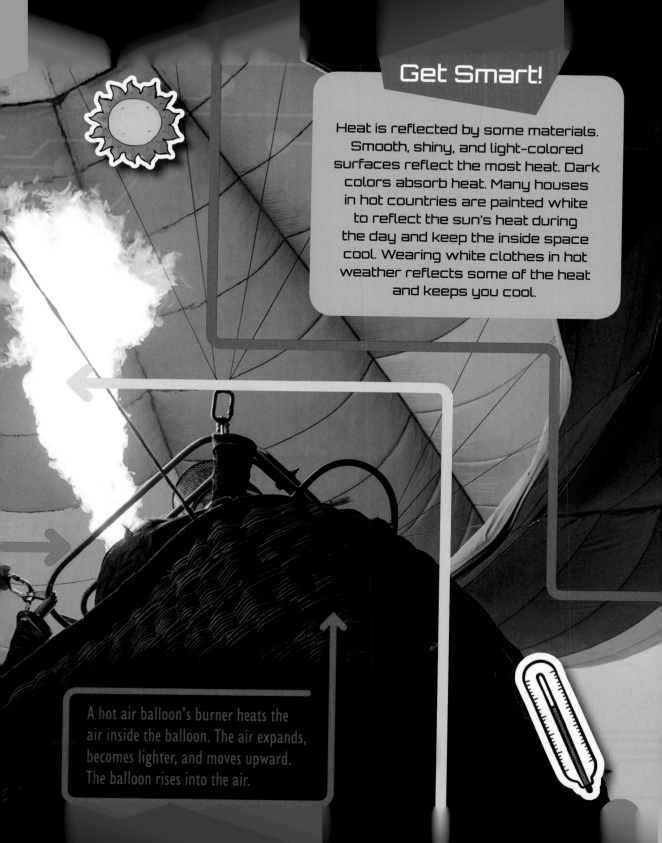

Get Smart!

Heat is reflected by some materials. Smooth, shiny, and light-colored surfaces reflect the most heat. Dark colors absorb heat. Many houses in hot countries are painted white to reflect the sun's heat during the day and keep the inside space cool. Wearing white clothes in hot weather reflects some of the heat and keeps you cool.

A hot air balloon's burner heats the air inside the balloon. The air expands, becomes lighter, and moves upward. The balloon rises into the air.

Good insulators keep you warm when it's cold outside and cool when it is hot. Solids, liquids, and gases can all be good insulators. Air is a good insulator. Layers of material that trap air between them are often used to stop the flow of heat.

In a building, the roof and windows are the areas that let the most heat in or out. In cold places, layers of insulating material are placed below the roof, and windows are made of two or even three layers of glass with a space between them. In hot parts of the world, many traditional homes have small windows to keep the inside cool, or the windows might be shaded with shutters.

In the past, wool was one of the warmest fabrics and people wore heavy knitted sweaters in winter. Today, synthetic fleece jackets and sweatshirts are much lighter and warmer. Thermal underwear is also made of synthetic materials and insulates your body, arms, and legs. People who live and work in cold places make sure to keep their head, feet, and hands insulated too.

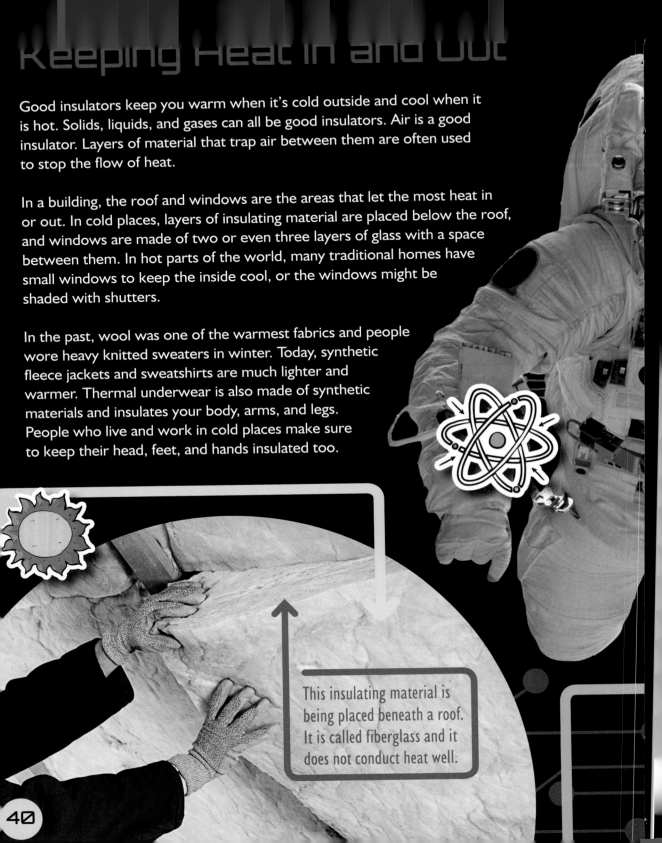

This insulating material is being placed beneath a roof. It is called fiberglass and it does not conduct heat well.

40

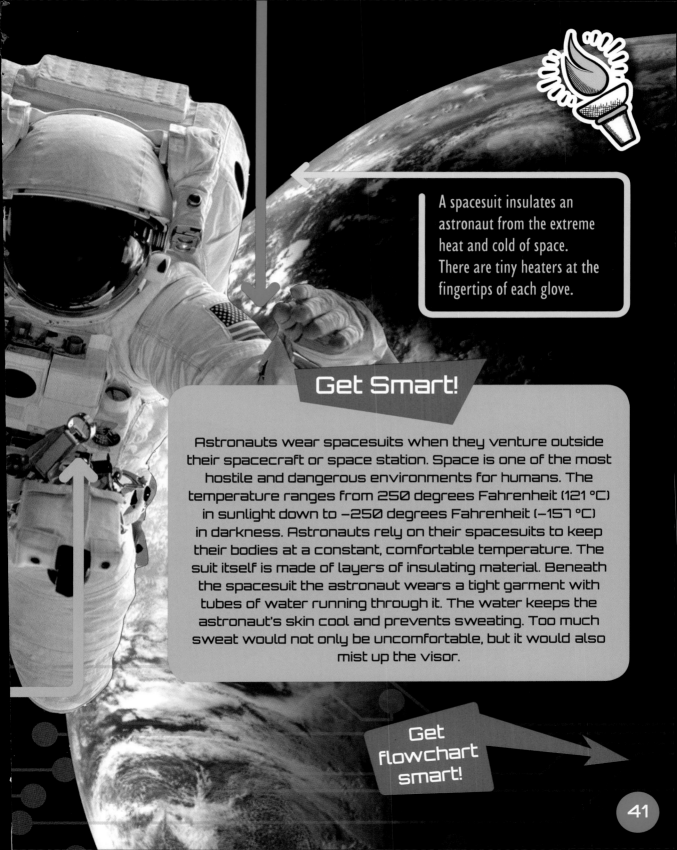

A spacesuit insulates an astronaut from the extreme heat and cold of space. There are tiny heaters at the fingertips of each glove.

Get Smart!

Astronauts wear spacesuits when they venture outside their spacecraft or space station. Space is one of the most hostile and dangerous environments for humans. The temperature ranges from 250 degrees Fahrenheit (121 °C) in sunlight down to –250 degrees Fahrenheit (–157 °C) in darkness. Astronauts rely on their spacesuits to keep their bodies at a constant, comfortable temperature. The suit itself is made of layers of insulating material. Beneath the spacesuit the astronaut wears a tight garment with tubes of water running through it. The water keeps the astronaut's skin cool and prevents sweating. Too much sweat would not only be uncomfortable, but it would also mist up the visor.

Get flowchart smart!

How Heat Spreads

Follow the flowchart to see how a spacesuit controls the temperature of an astronaut's body.

SUCCESS

The white outer layer of a spacesuit reflects the intense energy radiating from the sun.

Gloves are filled with air to insulate the astronaut's hands and fingers.

Flowchart
Smart

The thick suit is made of several layers of insulating fabric, including Gore-Tex, Dacron, and neoprene. These materials prevent heat from entering or leaving the suit and keep the internal temperature constant.

Tubes of water inside the astronaut's undergarment take heat away from the skin and prevent the astronaut from sweating heavily. Without these tubes, sweat would condense on the visor and obscure vision.

Energy Is
Never Lost

Energy can move from one place or substance to
another, and it can change form. For example, heat
can change into light or movement. Other types
of energy, such as electricity, can change into heat.
When a hot object cools, the energy is not lost, but
instead spreads into the surrounding environment,
warming a room or dispersing through the air.

Heat and light energy are closely linked. When
a substance burns, it creates light and heat. Very
high temperatures produce white light, and cooler
temperatures produce a yellow light. Light from the sun
and stars is produced by burning gases. The energy from
distant stars takes millions of years to reach Earth, but the
energy is not lost, it just spreads through the universe.

Movement energy can produce heat. Some of the energy of a moving object is converted to heat, particularly when one object slides across another. When you rub your hands together, the friction between them warms your skin. When a car makes a sliding turn, the tires heat up so much they can burn, producing clouds of smoke.

Most large power stations use heat to make electricity. Coal-fired and gas-fired power stations burn fuel to boil water and then use the pressure of the steam to spin a turbine. The energy of the moving turbine is converted into electricity. You can see how energy is in constant use in your own home—electricity is converted into heat in ovens and dishwashers, and into light, sound, and movement in household appliances. Energy is truly never-ending!

Massive amounts of fuel are burned in a coal-fired power station to generate electricity. During the process, steam is produced. These wide cooling towers are releasing the steam into the atmosphere.

Electricity powers tablets and other digital devices. They convert electricity into light and a little heat.

Friction between the car tires and the road produces heat and clouds of smoke.

Glossary

absolute zero the lowest possible temperature

atoms the smallest particles of a pure substance, such as oxygen, hydrogen, or carbon. Atoms join together to make molecules.

carbohydrates the main types of food that the body uses to get energy

combustion combining with oxygen by burning

condenses cools and changes from a gas into a liquid

conduction the process by which heat moves from one object to another through direct contact

conductors materials through which heat moves easily

contracts shrinks and takes up less space

convection the process in which heat is carried by a moving liquid or gas

convection current a circular stream in a liquid or gas that carries heated molecules upward where they cool and sink back to be heated again

energy the ability to do work or to make something change or happen

evaporate to change from a liquid into a gas

expand to become larger and take up more space

freeze to change from a liquid to a solid

insulators the materials through which heat cannot pass easily

molecule the smallest particle of a substance that can exist and still have the properties of that substance

precipitation when water vapor condenses and falls as rain, sleet, snow, or hail

protein large molecules made of amino acids that are an essential part of all living organisms

radiation the process by which heat is transferred across a space

reversed changed back to the way it was before

state of matter whether a substance is a solid, liquid, or a gas. Heating and cooling can change the state of matter.

sublimation the process in which a solid changes directly to a gas, without first becoming a liquid

temperature a measure of the amount of heat in a substance, usually measured in Fahrenheit or Celsius

thermometer an instrument for measuring temperature

troposphere the lowest layer of air in the atmosphere

unpasteurized not treated by heating to kill germs

vibrate to shake rapidly back and forth

water cycle the endless process in which water evaporates from the surface of Earth into the air, where it condenses to form water that falls back to Earth

For More Information

Books

Biskup, Agnieszka. *The Solid Truth about States of Matter with Max Axiom Super Scientist* (Graphic Science). Chicago, IL: Capstone, 2009.

Brent, Lynnette. *States of Matter* (Why Chemistry Matters). New York, NY: Crabtree Publishing, 2008.

Magloff, Lisa. *Experiments with Heat and Energy* (Cool Science). New York, NY: Gareth Stevens, 2010.

Stewart, Melissa. *Water* (National Geographic Readers). Washington, DC: National Geographic, 2014.

Websites

Read this easy-to-follow website to find out all you want to know about states of matter:
idahoptv.org/sciencetrek/topics/matter/facts.cfm

Visit this website to see which chemicals create which colors in fireworks:
scifun.chem.wisc.edu/chemweek/fireworks/fireworks.htm

Discover 10 things you can use to put out a fire:
www.firescienceschools.org/blog/2010/10-things-you-can-use-to-put-out-fires

Find out how a spacesuit insulates and regulates heat and keeps an astronaut alive in space:
www.nasa.gov/audience/forstudents/5-8/features/what-is-a-spacesuit-58.html

Publisher's note to educators and parents: Our editors have carefully reviewed these websites to ensure that they are suitable for students. Many websites change frequently, however, and we cannot guarantee that a site's future contents will continue to meet our high standards of quality and educational value. Be advised that students should be closely supervised whenever they access the Internet.

Index